Praise for *Terminal Maladies*

"Because the growl of thunder was distant," the speaker notes in *Terminal Maladies*, "I completely ignored it." The mere mention of the far-off rumbling, however, means otherwise. This thunderous collection considers the space between attention and abstraction, between life and death. Which is another way to say *love*.

—Nicole Sealey, author of *The Ferguson Report: An Erasure*

Okwudili Nebeolisa's debut, *Terminal Maladies*, introduces a poet so skillful and original that his book represents a vital moment in contemporary poetry. Centering around the loss of the poet's mother, these poems match acute observation with abiding sympathy. Masterful with formal as well as free verse, Nebeolisa moves beyond mere technique: His lines and sentences render the people he portrays with agile care. They also reveal, with often disarming immediacy, a writer capable of remaining in uncertainty and still determined to face unanticipated, often painful truths. Unsparing and yet infinitely tender, these are major poems. They will be with us for a long time to come.

—Peter Campion, author of *One Summer Evening at the Falls*

Okwudili Nebeolisa's *Terminal Maladies* is an unflinching debut wrought by the power of naming, the power of image, a mother's belief in the power of prayer. Clear-eyed but abashed, this collection insists on the necessity of memory and the inevitability of elegy. Nebeolisa's speaker is at once vulnerable and indifferent, yet I felt undone by the speaker's love for mother and depth of feeling for home no matter the distance.

—Donika Kelly, author of *The Renunciations*

Terminal Maladies is a book measured in distance from mother—our first other. In these heartfelt but unerringly unsentimental poems, birth, the differentiation of self, migration, and death are plotted as points along a continuum; the émigré's geographic separation from his ailing mother presages the ultimate, unfordable one, just as the poet's estrangement of syntax mirrors interior dislocations. Okwudili Nebeolisa is a poet of subtlety and surprise, in whose voice his mother's, on the other end of the line, still reverberates.

—Jameson Fitzpatrick, author of *Pricks in the Tapestry*

TERMINAL MALADIES

TERMINAL MALADIES

OKWUDILI NEBEOLISA

AUTUMN
HOUSE PRESS
Pittsburgh, PA

Cover and Book Design: Melissa Dias-Mandoly
Cover Art: *Sleeping Ariadne*. Roman art, 2nd century AD. Held at Florence National
Archaeological Museum. Image Courtesy of Gabinetto Fotografico delle Gallerie
degli Uffizi.
Author Photo: Otosirieze Obi-Young

Library of Congress Cataloging-in-Publication Data

Names: Nebeolisa, Okwudili, author.
Title: Terminal maladies / Okwudili Nebeolisa.
Description: Pittsburgh, PA : Autumn House Press, 2024.
Identifiers: LCCN 2023057890 (print) | LCCN 2023057891 (ebook) | ISBN
   9781637680940 (paperback) | ISBN 9781637680957 (epub)
Subjects: LCGFT: Poetry.
Classification: LCC PS3614.E259 T47 2024 (print) | LCC PS3614.E259
   (ebook) | DDC 811/.6--dc23/eng/20240126
LC record available at https://lccn.loc.gov/2023057890
LC ebook record available at https://lccn.loc.gov/2023057891

This book was printed in the United States on acid-free paper that meets the
international standards of permanent books intended for purchase by libraries.

Autumn House Press is a nonprofit corporation
whose mission is the publication and promo-
tion of poetry and other fine literature. The
press gratefully acknowledges support from
individual donors, public and private founda-
tions, and government agencies. This book was supported, in part, by the Great-
er Pittsburgh Arts Council through its Allegheny Arts Revival Grant and the
Pennsylvania Council on the Arts, a state agency funded by the Commonwealth of
Pennsylvania.

Contents

after

home

EVENTUALLY

The night my older brother told me
that our mother had cancer, I cried

for so long and then I went to bed.
I dreamed that she had died. I woke up and cried.

If it happened in the dream, would calling it
trauma be apt? I buried my face

in the pillow so my brother who shared
the bed with me would not be aware.

My sister was the only one we had heard
cry that night. The rest of us, men, had looked

for quiet spaces in the bungalow,
somewhere we would not be found, somewhere

we could keep our masculinities intact.
But when I went to work the next morning,

I did not know how to tell my colleague
what I had heard last night. I buried my face,

sobbing, while he stood there, looking at me
as if I were a Norman Lewis painting.

I tried to contain my embarrassment
and almost suffocated myself;

I had refused to see the darkening clouds,
but now that the rain was here, it soaked everything.

PHANTOM HAIR

In the front yard, my mother and I
talked about a past in which she lived

without the cancer blossoming in her thigh,
a past in which she didn't know

that the mass would morph into cancer.
Mosquitoes bit our calves. I slapped and slapped,

but my mother, as she talked, bore the pain.
She has lived on the earth almost longer

with the growth than not—nursing it,
carrying it, like a prolonged pregnancy.

She looked up at the star-brimmed sky
as if it were not me she was talking to.

I looked up too: It was drab and cloudless.
She raised her hand to her bald head, stopping

so close to her scalp as if to touch
her imaginary hair. Without looking

at her, I could see her tingling fingers
searching for her cornrows that once were there.

MY FATHER'S CLOTHES

Because the growl of thunder was distant,
I completely ignored it, sitting
in the dining room with my mother
while she recalled a story about my father.
Dust ambled into the room, carrying
the news of rain. Even though she would travel
to Zaria the next day for her biopsy,
she had washed my father's clothes in the morning
and was now waiting for them to dry.

Clouds, dark and vast, congregated outside
so that through the open door you could see
the light green algae on the wall turn olive
and then, minutes later, into something ominous.
The wings of termites reflected the evening light.

What about the clothes we washed? she asked me,
limping from the sitting room to the front yard,
her gait lopsided, her right leg bending
to carry the weight away from the left.
Sit down, I said. *Let me bring in the clothes.*
But when has my mother ever listened?
Even with the pain, she hurried outside,
trying to move faster than the rain.
The growing dark swallowed her the way a grave
swallows a slowly lowered coffin.

ALL THE WRONG THINGS

In the dream, my mother pinned a camellia
to her hair—my mother, who would never

pin a flower to her hair; my mother,
who had just lost all of her hair to chemo.

She was wearing a tight dress that stopped
inches above her knees, showing the bulge

of the tumor in her thigh—my mother,
who would never wear a short dress,

who when the bulge in her thigh
started to announce itself,

would only wear long flowing bubas
or dress skirts with flounces that hid her.

She wouldn't stop smiling, and when I asked
what it was making her smile, she replied

that she, too, was unaware, but couldn't I
see that the sky was unusually blue—

my mother, who would never comment
about the weather except when it was

keeping her from attending a wedding
or walking to church in the morning.

After nights of insomnia and sleeping
during class, I had managed to sleep

while reading a book of poems—I, who
would never sleep, reading a book of poems.

KITCHEN SCENE

Mummy, maybe if you lie on your back,
the pain will not be as sharp.
Mummy, I caught you wincing. Mummy, sit.

She would not leave the kitchen
and let my sister prepare dinner.
While I led her back to the sitting room,
she stopped in the sunlight pouring
through the window in the door
to observe the chemo rash
on the back of her hand.

Tightening her grip on my lower arm,
I felt her move the weight of her body
from her bad thigh to the healthy one.
Holed up in the house, mostly in her bedroom,
watching Nigerian films, listening
to sermons, the sun hardly touched her body.
There was quiet on her side. She had begun
to snore. I adjusted her head on the headrest.

She woke up, coughing, dryly, like the sound
of maize seeds in the maws of a grinder.
I thought that, as usual, her throat was burning
and got her a glass of water. She would not drink.
She pushed my hand away, spilling the water
on my trousers and on the sofa.
It was the food in the kitchen, burning.
Because I was suffering from a cold,
I could barely smell the smoke.
Even in her sickness, even in her dreams,
my mother was still aware of the food
my sister was cooking. It was as if
she had left the sitting room
to enter the kitchen in her dream.

BREAKING MELON SEEDS WITH MY MOTHER

Seated on the floor, my mother and I
broke melon seeds for egusi soup.
Sunlight pooled in the bowl between us.
I helped her unclasp her bra,
and wind from the opened door unraveled
the heat in my mother's body.
Sweat rolled in rivulets down her chest,
pooling in her belly button.
The sugary smell of her sweat and cologne
saturated the sitting room.

She has learned many ways of sitting
in chairs, of sitting on the floor, ways
that would least trouble her femur, ways
that wouldn't press on the growth. One morning
she sat like a normal human being
and then struggled to stand up on her own.
I liked to watch my mother sitting, resting.
But the cancer in her thigh would wobble
under her dress as she tried to adjust her leg.
Did you see that vibration in my leg,
she asked, laughing. *It's the fluid moving.*

I think she must have been waiting for me
to laugh, but I merely squinted my eyes.
Sometimes my mother would make a joke
about her body, about what was happening,
expecting me to join her in laughing, but
when I didn't, she would remind me
that the growth had appeared in her thigh just
as her womb dilated to make room for me.

TAKING STOCK

Even with the growing weight in her leg,
my mother would go around the house,
every night, switching off the lights in each room,
unconsciously checking on the people
in her house, even though she had seen us all
before going to bed. Because she had grown up
with stories about evil spirits
impaling the bodies of sleeping children,
she always made sure to rearrange us
if we positioned ourselves
in the ways that would invite bad dreams.
Anytime I heard her heavy footfalls
heading for our bedroom, I'd pretend
to be asleep, tucking my neck and legs
in crooked ways, just to feel her hands
touch me as she gently pushed a pillow
to support my head, unfolded my legs,
and then pulled the blanket up to my neck,
disrupting her sleep to make sure ours wasn't.

SOLO JOURNEY TO GOD

You have probably seen my mother
on the street with her long rosary, praying,

on her way to church; the tall woman
who looks like she is talking to herself

but is actually talking to her God.
Every other morning, like that, waking us

for morning devotions, saying five decades
of the rosary before embarking

alone to the church, even after
she heard her friend was robbed

early one morning on her way to work.
I wish I could believe the same way

my mother believed in her God,
even when the cancer did not allow her

to walk and it did not seem God
was listening. I once asked her

if she cared that God was not answering
but she replied, *Even no is an answer.*

SITTING

Even with the tumor in her left thigh,
my mother did not mind doing
my father's laundry, sitting on a stool
and kneading out dirt with her knuckles
all morning, singing Catholic hymns as she worked
the narrow shelves of her clavicles.
We stopped trying to convince her
to let us help or telling her that my father
would still know that she loved him,
a polite joke we shared. I would wait
for her to roll her eyes and explain
to me again how my generation
did not know what it means to love someone.
And she would wait for me to roll my eyes.

By the time she would finish, the sun
had spread its brocade across the sky;
she would have to take both of my hands in hers
to lift herself up, heaving out a sigh.
Even in her flowing gown you could still catch
the bulge of the tumor in her left thigh.
Years and years of heeding the advice
of doctors not to excise the growth
had left her with this ripe pumpkin in her thigh.

Sitting was the only time it was hard
to find it on her body, the only time
she seemed to forget about the pain.
I imagined that every time she had
to stand, it was as if she were walking
into that familiar cathedral of pain.
Over the years she had only gotten
better at masking her pain, so good
that I no longer trusted her each time
I saw her lift herself from a chair,
clamping down on the armrest, smiling.

MONOLOGUE

I thought it was drool rolling down the side
of your mouth, but it was a trick of the light.
Maybe it was a smile. About to leave,
I thought I had heard someone say something.
But it was you, speaking in your dream.
Nestled in the sofa, your arm on your chest,
you were talking about your own mother.
I know I should have woken you—who knows,
maybe it was a nightmare, but your voice
was so gentle, so I listened.

Mama, Mama, just hear me out, you said.
The house you left is falling apart.
Because you said those words in Igbo,
they corralled an otherworldly meaning.
Mama, talk to me, you said. *All these men
you gave birth to are becoming helpless.*

This was my first time witnessing
the living calling on the dead for help.
I had thought it was something only diviners
did, in the night, summoning their ancestors
before a full moon, asking for advice.
Though I was not present in the dream
I could tell that Grandma was probably
not listening, the same way
most of the dead behave in dreams, dialogue
hardly being a two-way street when the dead
are among the pedestrians on it.

I COULD STILL HEAR HIM WHISTLING

My mother was tending to the garden
where she nurtured moringa, tomatoes,

spinach, and curry leaves. The climbers were
overrunning the neighbor's fence

because no one would attend to them.
She had brought it up but my father had kept on

whistling to himself, getting ready for work.
I tried to say a prayer over the din

of Father's Louis Armstrong record playing,
nursing a slight headache, my skull throbbing.

The Armstrong song drowned the words
of my prayer. Even after she stopped working

with her knife on the vines, I could still
hear her washing the excess leaves in a bath;

even after my father stopped the stereo
and left for work, I could still hear him whistling.

But was I not guilty as well, lying there in bed,
watching her clip the leaves of the climbers,

watching from the comfort of my bedroom,
even when I became aware that

I could ignore the pain in my head.

NOT SO SURE

One evening while my mother and I watched
a miracle session on Synagogue TV,
she laid her hand on her swollen thigh,
closed her eyes, and asked God to heal her.
Since the diagnosis, Synagogue TV
or any channel where a pastor
was casting out demons or healing the sick,
were the only channels my mother would watch,
just as I became engrossed by articles
about the kind of my mother's cancer
was discussed.

                Everyone had an opinion
about diet for cancer patients—
sometimes my mother liked to hear them
while she was cooking, making the kind of meals
the articles had told her not to eat.
But how could she just stop drinking Pepsi,
one of the few things that brought her happiness?
We had a date for her first chemotherapy session.
At the doctor's office, my sister said,
she sounded like she was eager to begin.

But now, looking at my mother mouthing
an inaudible prayer, her eyes closed,
I knew what my sister meant when we asked her
a second time if she was certain
that our mother was ready for the treatments,
and shrugging, my sister, her voice lapsing
into a whisper that betrayed her,
said that even though our mother wanted
to try out the chemo, it seemed like
she wanted to wait to see what God would do.

THE JOKE

Out of frustration at our complacency
with disorder, my mother liked to joke
that a day would come when she
would not be around to make sure

that dinner had been taken out of the fridge to thaw,
to wash my father's clothes, to wake me
every morning to prepare for work.
I still remember the night I came home

to an unusually quiet house,
the sitting room empty, the two candles
on my mother's altar casting long shadows
of the ceiling fan on the walls

and on the sofa, vaguely implying
that it had not been long since my mother
and sister finished saying their night devotion.
In her room, my sister was trying to smother her sobbing,

probably pressing her face into her pillow,
while my mother tried to console her:
Even though the doctors had labeled the growth
in her thigh as cancer, my mother said,

it did not mean she was going to die.
There, in the darkness of my sister's bedroom
while my mother told her to stop crying,
I could already imagine the house

without our mother in it: the sitting room
littered with my books, my brother's shoes,
my father's newspapers, all of us unable to sleep,
the house a mango savagely eaten to its kernel.

abroad

METASTASIS

In the brief video my friend had sent me,
I watched an umbrella-shaped tumor
—blue as cobalt, small as a poppy seed—
metastasize in the brain of a mouse,
like a gardenia unfolding at night,
seducing moths to stroke its stamen.

I wondered if my friend, a doctor,
had forwarded this recording to me
to let me know what could be happening
in my mother's hip: cancer mushrooming
from the muscle, resting its bulbous head
on her femur, latching its pollen-laden arm
to my mother's age-wearied tendon.

I had just told him the prognosis
of my mother's condition, laying the facts
out for his scrutiny. I watched the video again;
blue seeds colonized wiry terrains of red.
Was this what her doctor had meant when he said
that at a certain age the body puts up little resistance
even to antigens trying to conquer it?

Because I didn't want the video
to pronounce death for the mouse, I chose
to focus on the beauty occurring
throughout its small body, the theater
of the invasion: How had they achieved
such phosphorescence in a dying body?

NOMENCLATURE OF MY MOTHER'S PAIN

My mother is in ruins even though
she is putting up an appearance
that says the opposite. I don't want
to imagine the barb of pain in her thigh
when she tries to sit, when she tries to stand.
She can't walk a few feet without crouching,
without looking for someone to hold onto.
When she half admits that she could hardly stand
while she was at the market, I know
this is code that it is at its threshold,
that she is at a cliff and a puff of wind
could knock her off—*Mummy, talk about your pain.*
She has taken her third painkiller today.
She has an ulcer that new medications
won't allow to heal. Yet she will still fast.
Her son cannot ply the tiger's mouth
that is the Abuja-Kaduna expressway
without her express prayers. Her daughter
cannot be writing exams without God
being alerted of this precious time.
Her son needs a new job. Her niece
in Warri is dying. These people need praying.
She can never palm her rosary enough.
My mother comes back home needing a drink,
a sweating glass of Pepsi even though
it will feed the cancer in her thigh.
Her doctor permitted her a few sodas
in a week. I don't understand her smile
or why she would be submerged in pain
and wouldn't want to admit it.
Who did this to our mothers? What's the source
of their forbearance? I keep a plate
of food before her but she wants to know
if her daughter passed her exams.
Mummy, don't worry about that, just eat.
But she insists: *How was the exam?*

The doctor couldn't believe the results
of the CT scan were for a fifty-six-year-old,
was shocked at the strength of her heart.
When would they proceed with chemotherapy,
was the first thing my mother inquired.
She is so sure she will survive
the chemotherapy. The seed-like tumor
has been in her thigh for twenty-seven years,
why would we suddenly believe it could
snuff her out now, was it merely because
the doctors had bestowed on it a name?

THINGS MY MOTHER'S CHILDREN DID FOR HER

I only gave her money. When I left,
it was all I could give. My sister
slept with her for two nights at the hospital.
My older brother traveled for hours
to spend a night with her in Zaria.
My younger brother donated blood
when her blood was not enough.
She laughed when she called to tell me
that she was back for chemotherapy.
But the suppressed streak of fatigue
was unmistakable. It was night
on her side of the earth while
it was nearly afternoon where I was.
The doctors, ready to give my mother
my brother's blood, waited so she
could finish speaking to her son.

While I was packing to travel overseas,
I should have stolen a picture of her,
one when she was young, to remind me
of what she was like before she was sick.
*You could not look at your mother
and not turn around,* her friend,
now living in the US, had said.
I should have stolen pictures of her,
but then, I thought I was doing myself
a kindness. Now each memory is a picture
of my mother: bald, delicate, smiling,
visibly keeping her concerns to herself.

OPEN WINDOWS

My dear, leave the windows open, let in
the light; I'm not feeling well today.
Maybe it's the rain. My father, in his last days,
disliked this kind of day, would stay
in bed and drink hot ginger tea
to warm his heart; my father who
in the harshest harmattan would head out
to his yam farm. My dear, please hold my hand,
I cannot seem to stand on my own.
Chemo has undone my bowels;
I have to visit the toilet again.
All my meals will get cold; if I eat,
I may have to find someone to get me
out of the bed, walk me to the bathroom
and then get me back to the bedroom.

Everyone keeps saying I haven't come
to the end and I can only wonder about
the deficiencies of their best intents.
Do they not think I may want to rest
like my father, who struggled in bed,
who when I hurried in to save his life, said
I should allow him to die? Do they not think
that while I kneel before my bed, praying
day in day out, mumbling to myself, I may
be trying to unravel the code to life with the hope
that I will ironically find that of death?

BACKYARD, MORNING

Every morning you go about the house,
waking the people in it, and then prayer—
five decades of the rosary, readings
from the missal, a register of rituals.
Everyone else moves like they are walking
in the dark: shortsighted, groping, their hands
almost out, only you seem agile.

The light outside slowly filling the rooms—
what else is there but to fall in love with it,
be bewitched before it tapers off?
In the backyard, your tomatoes and spinach
are unhurriedly dying in the heat.
There is no mincing words as you go on
in that mild light, taking them one by one.
Even the dogs know when their masters die.
Perhaps it is something in the air,
something with ethereal teeth, terminal.
The backyard is so bare it mirrors the sky.

TELEPHONE CONVERSATION

My mother still has me in her prayers,
even though she's the one who needs praying.
She still sees me in her dreams. Even though
I don't see her in mine. Over the phone,
I listened to her explain to me
how she could not sit after weeks of radiotherapy.
Her backside had peeled. Two mornings ago,
struggling to walk to the bathroom, she fainted,
and my brother, crying, beat her chest
till she resurfaced from the lagoon
of the dead. My father wept, imagining
this was how he would turn a widower.
Unable to sit on her backside,
she must have lain on her stomach for days—
enough to believe that she was floating.
She laughed, softening the seriousness
of her words—the ripple of her laughter
so loud I pulled out my earbuds.
Even though my airtime was ebbing,
I listened to her talk about mundane things:
how she ate bread, nibbling on it
for a long time before swallowing;
how she waited for one kind of pain
in one part of her body to relay
to another kind of pain in another
part of her body—sharp needles sprawling
to supernovas, one bolting through, the other rattling.
Where had she learned the word *supernova*?
Even the way it sounded on her tongue,
it was clear it was not part of her
natural vocabulary—it must have been
the news, maybe in a movie. I muffled
my laughter but it still tumbled out
from the cavernous tunnel of my mouth.
I did not want to describe the little things
I was enjoying in the US, the endless days
of uninterrupted electricity,

the taps that did not stop running even when
you were asleep, the possibility
that she would have received better care
if she were living here, that maybe
the doctors here would not have to transfer
her from one hospital to another.
I had let my mother talk; each time
we were on the phone, she would tell me
to forget about her—*Okwy tell me*
everything happening in the US—
as if my retelling would give her
the chance of another life.

THE PHOTOGRAPH

It was the first thing I saw that morning.
I had asked my younger brother
for a recent photograph of her.
A pearly dark had taken over her lips.
Even if she'd worn lipstick, you would still notice
the thick veneer of blackness beneath the sheen.
Her cheeks had hardened to two dark plums.
She was sitting on our old green sofa,
the sturdy cypress of her body, struggling
to survive, planted regally in the floral
pattern of her blouse. A cold prism of light
enclosed her like the image of angels
in a Botticelli painting.
She had not abandoned her posture,
sitting upright, looking away from the camera.
Before I had left Nigeria, I had seen
her fingers go so black they looked like talons.
Because there was no one else with me
in the room, I took the liberty to cry.
Maybe it was the darkness of the room
broadening my sorrow, like a phlox
unfurling under the moon's light.
Or could it be the time of the day, light
barely leaking from the cracked shell of dawn?
Music I'd listened to while sleeping
last night, floated by; the deep warm-hued voice
of the female singer drenching the room,
telling about the glories of her hometown
which she had become a stranger to.

MY OWN ASH

There was no body of water in this dream
but it must have been my ash in the urn
that my trembling lover was holding.
My mother was beside him in a neat coat
and stylish eyeglasses and high heels
that brought her head to the height of his chin.
I couldn't remember having this wish
or telling my lover to cremate me
—I used to think we would be grave-lovers.

I had always wanted for my relatives
to visit me after death. It was a ritual
for my mother to take me to her mother's grave
even though I had never met her—
though my mother strongly claimed otherwise—
she had died a few years after my birth.
The ash wasn't plentiful, the wind not strong
to buoy my many pieces across the patch
of grassland I was being flung onto.
My mother looked like someone who would rather
have been somewhere else and why was my lover
taking so long to shake off the urn's contents?
Perhaps waiting for the slightest of winds.
It was an expensive looking urn,
the kind of thing you would save to use
for another person's gray remains;
it must have been my mother's little gift,
the kind you give and expect to be returned.

MEMO

Call your mother, make her believe
that she is not desolate in her illness,
that while she thumbs her rosary in her room,
someone, rivers away, is listening.
Everyone kept on saying, before you left,
to always remember her, as if you could
forget the wet clay from which you were molded,
as if a gopher would forget its burrow
in the ground during a wildfire.
Tell her you remember how she mashed fried rice
with her fingers before putting it
in your mouth even though you don't remember.
Tell her you saw her in your dream last night
telling you a story in an idyllic setting.
Set the story in the land where she was born.
Listen to her sighs while you tell the story.
Pause for effect at every turn of the plot,
allow her to delight in it like a woman
relishes her first bowl of pepper soup
brimming with large chunks of fish and chicken,
after she has just given birth, the kind
of soup that is believed to seep into the womb
and heal the cracks, to make the room
habitable for another child.
You may have given a fine rendition
but don't cut the call yet. Be obedient, child.
She might not believe that you dreamed about her
but she will not say. Allow her to laugh.

TITHE

I listened to my mother describe
how the doctor, with a black marker,
drew a broken line across the growth
in her thigh. Explaining they would empty
the thigh of the mass the way a child
would scoop custard with a spoon.
The chemo and the radiation had not worked.
If too many muscles were undone,
my mother might end up unable to walk.
Because she was talking about her body
as if it were a piece of cutlery,
I wondered if she had started to give up.

Because I couldn't see her face, I couldn't
tell if she was afraid. She had acquired
a stoicism even soldiers would envy,
talking about her body as if
it were something that no longer belonged
to her but to medical specialists,
allowing them to make the decisions
about what procedures to carry out,
rendering the remnants of faith to God,
like a farmer who, despite being displeased
with the harvest, still gathers the one-tenth
of his profit in his best bushel basket.

AFTER THE RADIOTHERAPY

On the phone, I listen to my mother
narrate how, now, months after the "radio,"
she could board a motorcycle and head
to the market all by herself, something
she couldn't do before the chemo,
before I left, when she could no longer
pretend that ibuprofen could suppress the pain.
During the radio she could not sit
for about a month, her body unable
to contain anything she managed to eat.
Usually, she would tell me about
the neighbor whose daughter had been kidnapped
or the school that had been raided by bandits
who made away with several students.
Did I remember the seminary
in Kagoma? As if I had ever been
to Kagoma. Don't I remember
Bethel Baptist Secondary School?
Twenty-eight students were missing after
some gunmen visited. But today her voice
was happy like she was whenever
she was dressing up for church. Even though
the healing was not complete, even though
the growth in her left leg was still swelling.
To distract myself from all the kidnappings,
I would part the blinds with two fingers
and eye the neighbors on the balcony.
We were at the warm end of spring,
blades of bright green ryegrasses had started
to sprout between the gutters and the sidewalks,
a few pansies in the neighbor's front yards—
last night it rained so gently I almost
missed it when I looked through the window.
Are you there? My mother's voice rose.
In the background was my sister's voice
begging to speak to me for five minutes.
To assure her of my attention,

I asked her about the pain in her thigh,
even though I was aware that the pain
would still be there. Like anyone
who has had pain escort them for two decades,
she replied to me that she could not tell,
the kind of reply she casually gave
and none of us could tell how grave the pain was
until she couldn't bear it anymore.

PERSUASION

How do you convince your mother that cutting
her leg off to save her life is the right choice?
After the chemo- and radiotherapy,
it had become hard to convince her
to embark on another medical trip.
Even my father was secretly tired.
My brother would never acknowledge
that taking care of our mother was a task
he wished he would one day be released from.
Only my sister would gladly leave school
to sit with my mother in the hospital
if the situation presented itself again.

I stay quiet, disguised in thought, listening
to cars drive past on the street, remembering
the uncanny ways in which we are alike:
the individuality of our minds.
I would have used the absence of pain
to deliver my argument, but then,
I remember in my parents' bedroom,
the bottles of ibuprofen, the blister packets
of paracetamol, diclofenac, and the sachets
of aspirin tablets littering their vanity set
like bottles of cosmetics which,
when I was younger, I did not
understand were like the bottles of beer
a man would take to defer the pain.

BECAUSE

Because I was not certain if my mother
was getting any better, if the pain

was abating, if the swelling
was receding, if she was sleeping better

at night, especially because
we lived on different continents,

the guilt did not miss me. Sometimes, I hoped
it would and nursed a fresh guilt for hoping.

I just wanted her to talk about the things
she would have talked about if she didn't

have cancer. I wanted to hear
what it was like haggling prices for pieces of beef

at the market, tasting the garri
before deciding to buy, exchanging jokes

with the sellers so they would bring down the price.
I just wanted to know there was still

the possibility of us talking
about other things that wasn't the thing

that might eventually do her in.

after

ETIQUETTE

In the African store, eyeing a pyramid
of Peak Milk tins, I tried to remember
why the woman beside me looked familiar:
the dark woolly hair, the fair complexion.
We traded smiles, staring at each other,
two strangers warily looking for
common grounds fertile for dialogue.

The accent, she asked, *where is it from*?
Pure interest illuminated her eyes,
not the passive attempt to alienate.
While we exchanged words, sharing information
about each other, it registered:
She reminded me of my mother,
the version of my mother who had no tumor
to worry over, whose chemo
hadn't scraped off the hair on her head,
who only lives now in pictures.

Like people in the movies, we nearly
butted into each other and then
enacted the playful kind of dialogue
that bordered on flirting: *You can go ahead.*
No, I don't mind. Go ahead. As if
we both possessed all the time in the world,
as if we would be breaking a secret kind
of etiquette that only people
back home would have any knowledge of,
the kind from which there was no returning.

ESCAPING

When there was no money coming
into the house, I started to expect
that phone call almost every other week:
My mother on the line, asking how I was
and then the conversation would segue
into the state of affairs at home. After the chemo,
she couldn't make money anymore. Mostly,
she stayed at home, tending to her pain.
Sometimes I would listen to her describe
her ordeals, taking care of herself
as well as taking care of the house,
until I had forgotten where I was.

I would listen even though I could feel
mosquitoes latching onto my skin,
even though poison ivy covered the field
adjacent to the lake. Lamps lit up
the motel rooms, amber silhouettes moving
around in the lighted rooms, and even though
my legs were itchy, I did not go in
for fear that the other residents
in adjacent rooms would be listening.
I didn't tell her that these many worries
were why I had been desperate to leave
despite the peculiar threat of loneliness
of living in another country.

It was easier to remain quiet
and listen to my mother complain
than to explain my desire to leave them.
I licked the bite on the back
of my finger from which a mosquito
had finished sucking. The last time
I spoke with my older brother, I could hear
my father's sad inflections in his voice.

Since I was thirteen, since we moved from
the two-bedroom apartment into
a three-bedroom, since I became
aware that we were almost always drowning
in unpaid bills, unpaid fees, unpaid rent,
that it was my mom keeping us afloat,
I had always thought of escaping.

FACADE

Because I knew the call would be laced
with tragedies, I tried to keep it short,
aiming to trim it to its essentials—
either someone had been kidnapped or some bill
was waiting to be paid, unable to be paid,
or the pain in my mother's hip had worsened
or the wrong man had been sworn into office

or my father's business would have to face
some sort of foreclosure because of rent.
Sometimes there was a sprinkle of good news
but even that was met with suspicion.
I often pretended to be asleep;
many times, I apologized for the missed calls
but didn't call back. It was easier

to imagine the bad news than to hear it
from the mouth of someone I knew.
I blamed the missed calls on time zones,
effusively explaining how insomnia
had made it worse. I would be on my phone
when a message would beep but ignorance
was easier than acknowledgment—my dad,

asking for the third time that week
how my semester was panning out
even though I was on holidays.
I always, hours later, sometimes days later,
said I was fine even if an hour ago
I had buried my face in the sheets
hoping my flatmate would not hear me crying.

ORANGE

It was the summer I listened to my mom
describe the strange color of her urine,

the summer I binge-watched *Euphoria*
even though I was tired of seeing

twenty-something-year-old actors play the roles
of teenagers, even though I wondered

why the girls had nothing but boys on their minds,
why the boys had nothing but destroying girls

on their minds, why the director had used
strobe lights to highlight the makeup around their eyes.

It was the summer that my mother joked
about how even though it was months after

the chemo, her urine was still dark
no matter how much water she drank.

She was always drinking water.
Even on the phone. Her throat was dry.

Because I had laughed, she thought I didn't
believe her. *You should have smelled it,*

she said. *It was stronger than caffeinated sweat.*
She wanted to know what was playing

in the background. *Whose voices are those,* she asked.
It was Zendaya talking to Sydney.

I continued to laugh until she joined me—
because she joined me, I knew that she knew

that I completely believed her.

RETROSPECTIVE

After we had raised the money for radiotherapy,
we told ourselves that the tumor must have shrunk
to a size that radiation would easily smother it.
We talked about the dates more than we talked
about Christmas, which was merely weeks away—
they managed to purchase a whole chicken;
there had always been rice in the house.
My mother had recently shaved her head
just in case the radiation turned out
to be like chemo.
                              I didn't tell them
that I had traveled to Houston to see
a potential lover, that the other voice
in the adjacent room was his, hoping
that on the video call they wouldn't notice
the details of this room, how the walls
were different, how it did not contain
my bookcase, my bed littered with books.

I don't know how I would have fared
spending the winter all on my own,
receiving one piece of bad news after another.
Though I had a roommate, we lived our lives
like two people speaking separate languages.
It only made sense that when this man offered me
his company, I would immediately accept it.
Because we were still new to each other,
I did not let him know of the cancer
exploding in my mother's thigh; I'd learned
early on it was best not to overwhelm.
                              I did not want
anyone to start consoling me.
Sometimes it felt like I was telling a lie
by not revealing the truth.

Almost a year later, no longer in love
with this man, I looked back on the events
for hints of fracture, like anyone
trying to recover the missing details
of a dream: Had I been vain in ways that had
completely missed me?
                                For months, I didn't try,
as if I were waiting for my mother
to complete her medications, to call me
one day, bearing good news.
                                        I didn't try
to reconcile with the man in Houston.
One year of following my mother's illness
had robbed me of the capacity
to react to things that were not about her—
one moment I'm closing my eyes to the thrill
of a wriggling tongue on my nipple
and the next I would suddenly remember.

THE BLEEDING STORY

Even an anemic person would not bleed
like that, the blood would just not stop;
there shouldn't have been any need
for the bandage. The nurse had assured her
that by the time she got home she could remove
the dressing and throw it away,
but the wound continued to weep.
There was no plaster at home to stop it.

My brother pressed a ball of cotton to the wound,
tied it with a sock, and waited. And waited.
My brother did not know what to do.
She tried to sleep, to ignore the bleeding—
even people with cancer have other lives
to live, have other dreams to dream.
She liked to tell me this story whenever
she remembered it. And she liked to laugh
when she finished telling it.

SURVIVAL

For a long time, my sister was her nurse
when my brother could no longer sit
beside her, waiting for her to need help.
My sister, studying to be a nurse,
had naturally picked up the role.

When I asked my brother what it had been like,
he would not reply it was a relief.
We went down the dark road
of abstraction. Some nights, he had to sneak out
of the house to meet some friends at the bar.
Most of the time, he said, *she was sleeping.*
He didn't have to tell her he was going out
or she would demand some specificity.

My sister refused to go into
the particulars of taking care of her
since much about it was dirty.
She said there were days she sang to her
like a baby. *To her,* she said, *not for her.*
After a painful silence, she added:
The person taking care has to survive.

FAITH, BUT NOT AS A METAPHOR

I walked down the cobbled street of North Linn,
thinking about the phone call I'd had
with my mother earlier that day.
It was mid-May.
                  Graduation was in swing.
Students partied in their basements. Sometimes,
a drunk student would run out of a house, laughing,
holding a beer bottle, banging the door
behind him, rushing toward the road
before heading back into the house.
I had carried on with my life for the whole day,
singing while I did the dishes in the sink,
while I fed clothes into the dryer,
while I folded the clean clothes, made the bed,
as if I hadn't heard that the two years
of chemo and radio did not work,
that to remove my mother's infected leg
from her body was their final recourse.

All through the conversation, my mother
had tried to skirt around the topic—
if she had wanted it, she would have said it.
If she had wanted it, she would have given me
a likely date for the surgery.
                      Her silence
implied that she wanted to wait.
We continued to talk about miracles.
For my mother, faith would never be
a metaphor, the kind of thing that derived
meaning from being likened to another.
I have to tell myself that she will keep
believing in her God even after
he has repeatedly failed her—
if she made it out alive, she would thank her God
instead of the doctors.

Faith was the sort
of thing that had the power to transcend life,
like a radioactive element leaking
radiation for all of eternity.

LITANY OF REMEDIES

Trying to heal herself, my mother had tried
drinking half a cup of raw quail eggs,
soya bean milk, juice extracts;
chewing moringa leaves, ground moringa seeds;
eating grapefruits; fasting long hours; interpreting
her dreams to see if healing was imminent.
One time, a friend suggested she try drinking urine.
She hopped from one charlatan to the next,
kneeling before their feet so they could lay
their hands on her head and cast out the pear-sized
tumor in her thigh.
                                    You need to hear her
talk about the new remedy her friend
with no medical experience had told her to try,
something they had plucked from the internet.
Or the new pastor on the adjoining street
performing miracles every other week.

I could not tell her that they wouldn't work.
It seemed like unintentional mockery.
My brothers tried not to talk about it.
After the chemo and the radio,
her hair began to grow back, and I could see
that she wanted that to be a good sign.
I too wanted that to be a good sign.
She and my brother drove more than 500 miles
to a pastor who could not heal her.

Toward the end of a phone call, she told me
how this young man, another pastor,
had tried to obligate her to pledge
money that she did not have, and so,
she took her purse, hooked it under her arm,
and left.

She was angry then, but now
retelling the story, reliving the details,
she laughed as if amused at herself,
at the person she was subtly becoming.

SUBTLETIES

Explaining to my mother that I would not
be traveling back to Nigeria

within the next five years,
I waited for her to ask a second time

about my plans after graduation.
Maybe postgraduate studies, I said.

She *hmmm*ed and *hmmm*ed, taking in
the implication of my reply, trying

to accept not being able to see
one of your children for that long.

When, in my mind, I had played how the incident
would go, I had expected her to ask me:

What if she had passed before I came back,
what if the cancer did not pity her?

We had passed the blame around for a while—
my father's fault, my fault, maybe it was

my mother's? I did not believe that time
would weaken the band of yearning I wore

when I left them. We were a family
used to employing subtleties with the hope

that the recipient would translate these tics.
My sister was singing in the background,

her voice scraped clean with a strange happiness
until my mother tersely told her to shut up.

SIMPLICITY

Unlike me, she wanted the simplest things.
Electricity to keep her soup in the fridge,
money to keep the landlord from knocking.
Even though I was in another continent,
I would sometimes imagine her praying
for the dark amber stain of the chemo
to drain from the tips of her fingers,
for the tingly feeling to disappear.
After some time, she stopped begging God
to make the cancer vaporize from her leg.

Not even the doctor could wrest her hand
from a bottle of Pepsi.
                              She didn't care
if her husband was not in bed by the time
she was retiring for the day—
sometimes she wanted the bed to herself.
I had seen that when my father traveled.
It was not pretense.
                           Her love had escaped
the borders of worry and walked into
the field of indifference. One time I tried
to mirror her modest desires,
telling her how I merely wanted
a roof over my head, a fridge with food
enough to feed me for several days,
and money enough to stave the worry
for at least a month.
                            But she remained quiet
for an uncomfortable length of time,
a silence I had come to learn
was her politest form of disagreement.

SAVINGS

Sometimes I would keep aside money
in case my mother called or sent a text,

describing how things were hard at home—
radiotherapy did not improve her walking.

If she couldn't walk to church, then clearly
it was that bad. But it was summer,

and I did not get the fellowship.
Frugality did not help; cutting down

on dinner dates, coffee orders, does not
save anyone from the drought. One time,

I ordered myself a meal so expensive
the guilt forced me to laugh, as I remembered

my mother who had not worked for three years.
The man I had gone on a date with

kept on asking me what it was,
but I would not answer. Something about

the look of confusion on his face
told me I would not see him again.

DECOY

It had been three years since the night we found out
my mother had been living with cancer.

She was still alive. I have marked every year
I've lived in the US as a triumph.

I did not know why I brought it up
on a first date, as if I were begging

the man to commiserate with me.
Our orders hadn't even arrived.

It was so loud in the restaurant
that he asked me to come again, but how do you

say, for the second time, on a first date,
that your mother has been living with cancer

for years? So, unbuckling the second top button
of my shirt, just where the tiny prickly hairs

sprouted out of my chest, I sighed, looking
to see if he would fall for the decoy.

SECRECY

I remember telling my mother
that I had begun to write about her illness,
hoping she would get enraged, expecting
she would ask me why, half-wanting her

to forbid me from publishing the poems.
When I was young, she had warned us
never to tell anyone anything about
what was happening at home. For weeks

after the diagnosis, we did not tell,
waiting for her to do the rendering:
Even after she had told her sisters,
she didn't want my father to tell even his folks.

I had prepared myself to tell her
that the poems were just an experiment,
that I was not planning to publish them.
And when I finally told her

about the project, I was surprised
to hear something like defeat in her voice
as she asked if there was anything else
I wanted to know about her suffering.

THE LAST THING

The last thing my mother asked for,
before she passed, was food. My brother left the room

to obey her request. By the time he came back,
she had left. As if she did not want to do

the business of dying in his presence,
like a parent distracting their toddler

with a toy before sneaking out of the house.
She would not let him see her go. By the time

he was back, her eyes were closed
as if she were just momentarily dozing,

her body warm as an ember glowing
in the dark charcoal bed of a grill.

Nkoli Georgina Nebeolisa
(January 23, 1964 – July 23, 2023)

ACKNOWLEDGMENTS

Most of these poems were written in isolation, so I don't know where to start, but I'm grateful to my mom, Nkoli Nebeolisa, who permitted me to write about this, who fed me with stories. This book would not have been written without my siblings, Tobe, Dubem, Nneka, and finally my dad, Donatus Nebeolisa.

I remain eternally grateful to the Center for African American Poetry and Poetics (CAAPP) at the University of Pittsburgh and to Nicole Sealey for giving my project a chance. I have to acknowledge every first reader who read entries for the CAAPP Book Prize and passed my manuscript over to the *yes* pile. And to my editor, Christine Stroud, for her generous contributions.

I wrote at least 50 percent of this book at the Artist Residency at Lakeside Lab, abandoning the project I proposed to work on (nature poems) and rather writing first drafts of the poems that made it into this book. I don't know if I would have done this book if I wasn't brooding as I stared at Lake Okoboji and wondering what to do with my life. I remain thankful to all the staff and the interns who keep that place alive.

I am filled with gratitude to the Granum Foundation who provided me with financial support to write parts of this book.

I'm indebted to these two women who have supported me at different points in my career: Prof. Jenny Davidson and Ellah Wakatama (OBE).

For supporting this book and my work, for your kind words, thank you Dr. Donika Kelly, Prof. Peter Campion, and Prof. Jameson Fitzpatrick.

I can't express how thankful I am to the Iowa Writers' Workshop (IWW) for giving me two years of ample time to solely think and write and make friends. I'm grateful to the poetry faculty—Profs. Elizabeth Willis, Tracy Morris, and Jim Galvin.

I remain grateful to Profs. Mark Levine and Lan Samantha Chang for your guidance and encouragement and for making my time at the IWW memorable. I'll forever remain your student.

I want to thank to my friends for your encouragement and for making the loss bearable: Jim Moore, Hussein Ahmad, Benedicta Esione, hurmat kazmi, Bhion Achimba, Cheta Igbokwe, Anthony Hendricks.

And finally, to these editors of these journals for publishing some of the poems in this book: Adam Day (*Action, Spectacle*), Melissa Crowe (*Beloit Poetry Journal*), Kristin George Bagdanov (*Ruminate Magazine*), Jessica Faust (*The Southern Review*), and Wendy Lesser (*The Threepenny Review*).

About CAAPP

The Center for African American Poetry and Poetics' (CAAPP) mission is to highlight, promote, and share the work of African American and African diasporic poets and to pollinate cross-disciplinary conversation and collaboration. Housed at the University of Pittsburgh, CAAPP's programming aims to present live poetry and conversation, contextualize the meaning of that work, and archive it for future generations.

The Center emerged in a 2015 brainstorming session between poets Dawn Lundy Martin, Terrance Hayes, and Yona Harvey, and was officially founded in 2016. Today, the Center is a space for innovative collaboration between writers and other artists, scholars, and social justice activists thinking through poetics as a unique and contemporary movement. In its effort to highlight, promote, archive, research, and generally advance the practices and epistemologies of African American and African diasporic poetry and poetics, CAAPP supports individual writers, artists, scholars, and others nationally and at a range of career stages and academic ranks. The Center also prioritizes providing opportunities for poets and artists outside of academia, in the Pittsburgh community and beyond.

About the CAAPP Book Prize

Started in 2020, the CAAPP Book Prize is a publishing partnership between CAAPP and Autumn House Press with the goal of publishing and promoting a writer of African descent. The prize is awarded annually to a first or second book by a writer of African descent and is open to the full range of writers embodying African American, African, or African diasporic experiences. The book can be of any genre that is, or intersects with, poetry, including poetry, hybrid work, speculative prose, and/or translation.

NEW AND FORTHCOMING FROM AUTUMN HOUSE PRESS

Book of Kin by Darius Atefat-Peckham

Winner of the 2023 Autumn House Poetry Prize,

selected by January Gill O'Neil

Near Strangers by Marian Crotty

Winner of the 2023 Autumn House Fiction Prize,

selected by Pam Houston

Deep & Wild: On Mountains, Opossums & Finding Your Way in West Virginia by Laura Jackson

Winner of the 2023 Autumn House Nonfiction Prize,

selected by Jenny Boully

Terminal Maladies by Okwudili Nebeolisa

Winner of the 2023 CAAPP Book Prize,

selected by Nicole Sealey

I Have Not Considered Consequences: Short Stories by Sherrie Flick

The Worried Well by Anthony Immergluck

Winner of the 2024 Rising Writer Prize,

selected by Eduardo C. Corral

Rodeo by Sunni Brown Wilksinson

Winner of the 2024 Donald Justice Poetry Prize,

selected by Patricia Smith

For our full catalog please visit: http://www.autumnhouse.org